Mel

GUITAR
288 Chords by .

2 # CONTENTS

TUNING THE GUITAR

The six open strings of the guitar will be of the same pitch as the six notes shown in the illustration of the piano keyboard. Note that five of the strings are below the middle C of the piano keyboard.

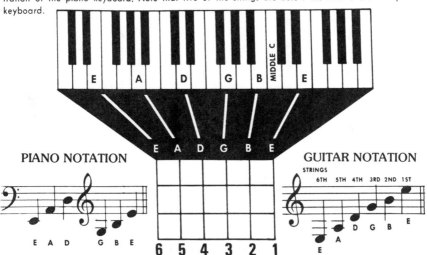

PIANO NOTATION

GUITAR NOTATION

ANOTHER METHOD OF TUNING

1. Tune the 6th string in unison to the E or twelfth white key to the LEFT of MIDDLE C on the piano.

2. Place the finger behind the fifth fret of the 6th string. This will give you the tone or pitch of the 5th string. (A)

3. Place finger behind the fifth fret of the 5th string to get the pitch of the 4th string. (D)

4. Repeat same procedure to obtain the pitch of the 3rd string. (G)

5. Place finger behind the FOURTH FRET of the 3rd string to get the pitch of the 2nd string, (B)

6. Place finger behind the fifth fret of the 2nd string to get the pitch of the 1st string. (E)

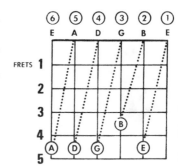

PITCH PIPES

Pitch pipes with instructions for their usage may be obtained at any music store. Each pipe will have the correct pitch of each guitar string and are recommended to be used when a piano is not available.

LEFT HAND FINGERING

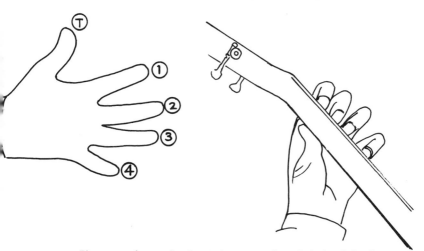

Place your fingers **firmly** on the strings **directly behind the frets.**

GUIDE TO CHORD DIAGRAMS

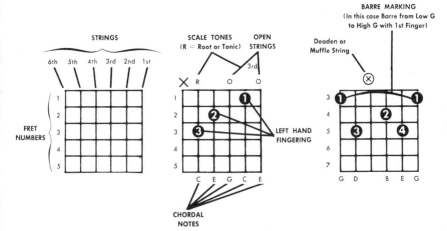

$\times$ = Do Not Play String

CHORD SYMBOL ABBREVIATIONS

Major = C, F, G, etc.   Dominant Seventh = C_7, F_7, etc.

Minor = Cm, Fm, etc.   Sixth = C_6, F_6, etc.

Diminished = $C°$, Cdim, C−, etc.   Minor 7th = Cm_7, Fm_7, etc.

Augmented = C+, C aug, etc.   Minor 6th = Cm_6, Fm_6, etc.

Major 7th = Cma_7, C_7

Dominant Seventh Sharp Fifth = C_7+5, $C_7\sharp5$, etc.

Dominant Seventh Flat Fifth = C_7-5, $C_7\flat5$, etc.

Ninth = C_9, F_9, etc.

Sixth Add Ninth = C9/6, F9/6, etc.

Seventh Suspended Fourth = C_7sus4, F_7sus4, etc.

Eleventh = C_{11}, F_{11}, etc.

Augmented Eleventh = $C_{11}+$, $F_{11}+$, etc.

Thirteenth = C_{13}, F_{13}, etc.

A

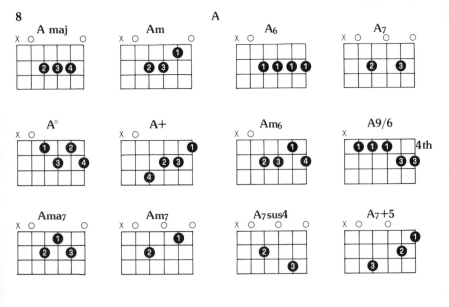

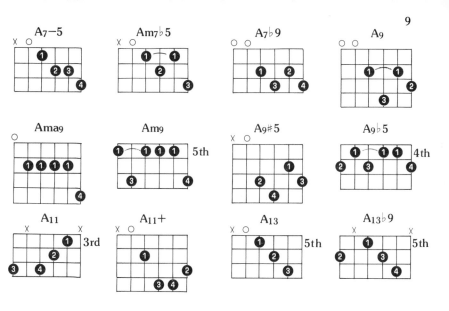

A#/B♭

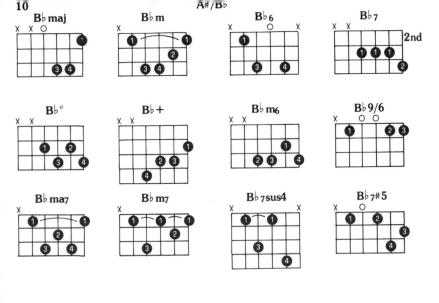

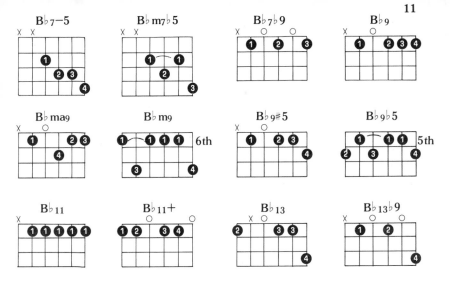

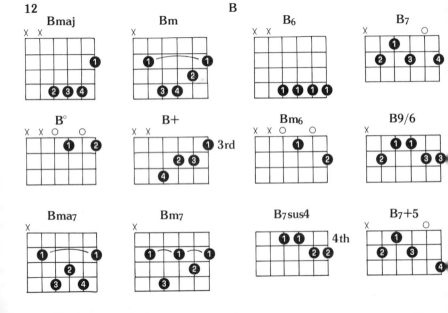

B7−5
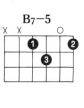

Bm7♭5

B7♭9

B9

Bma9

Bm9

B9♯5

B9♭5
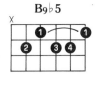

B11
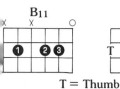

B11+

T = Thumb

B13

B13♭9

C

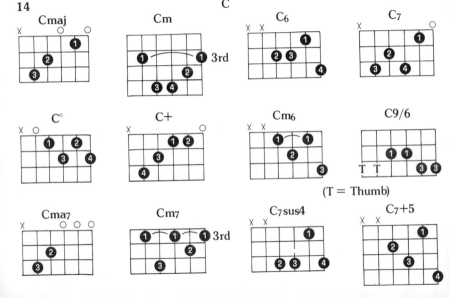

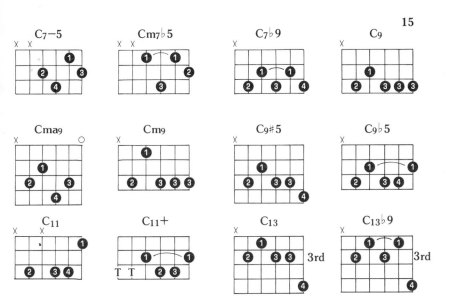

C#/Db

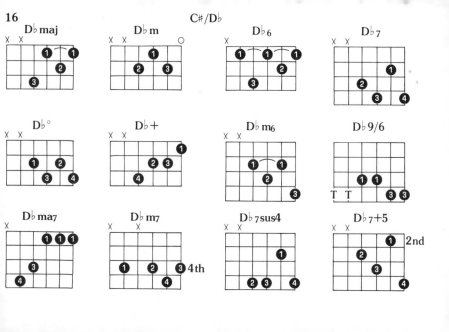

Db maj

Db m

Db 6

Db 7

Db °

Db +

Db m6

Db 9/6

Db ma7

Db m7

Db 7sus4

Db 7+5

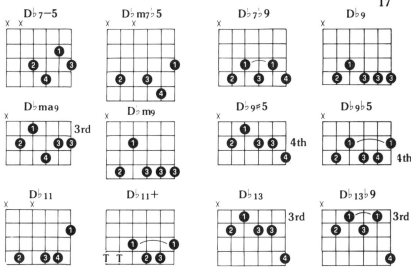

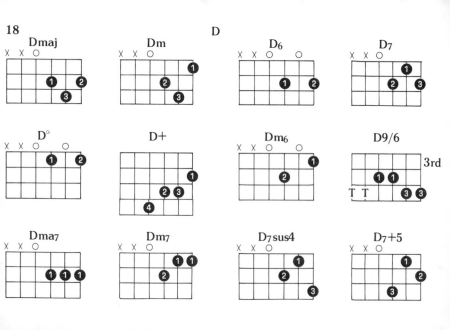

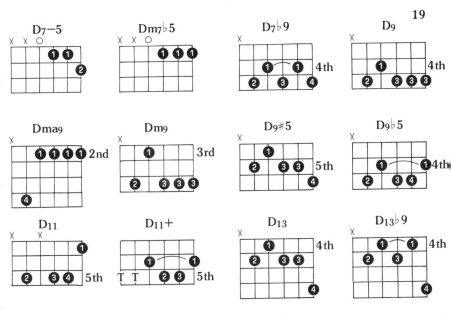

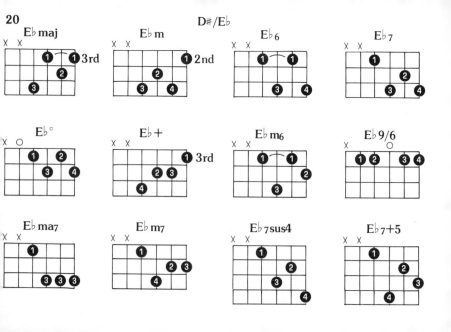

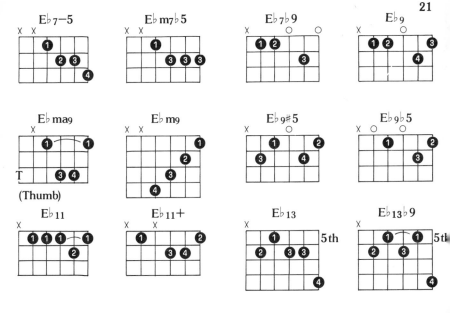

E

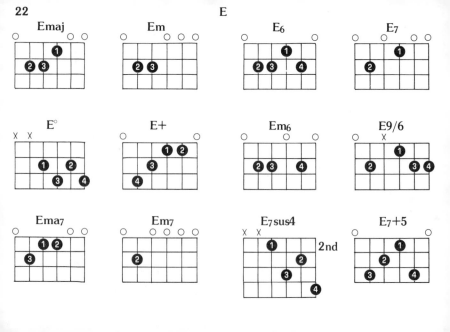

Emaj   Em   E6   E7

E°   E+   Em6   E9/6

Ema7   Em7   E7sus4   E7+5

2nd

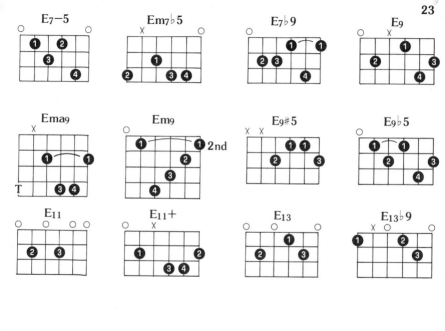

F

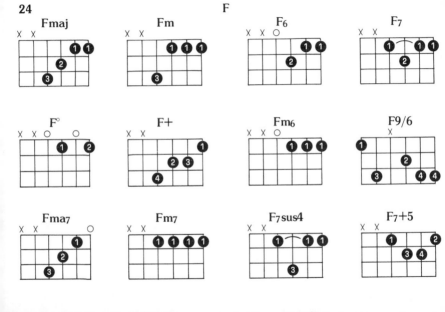

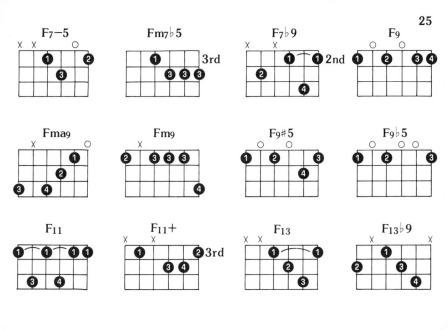

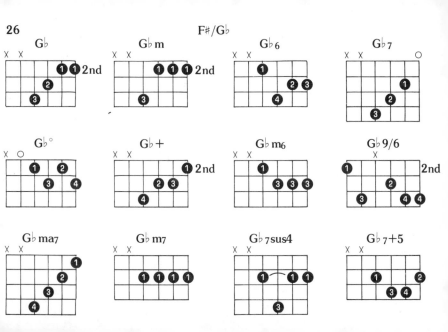

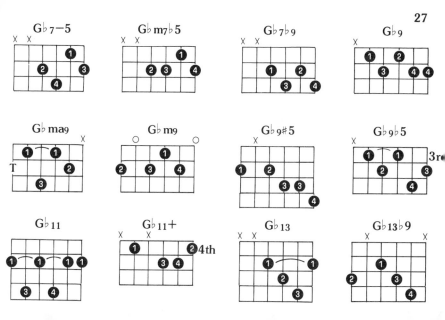

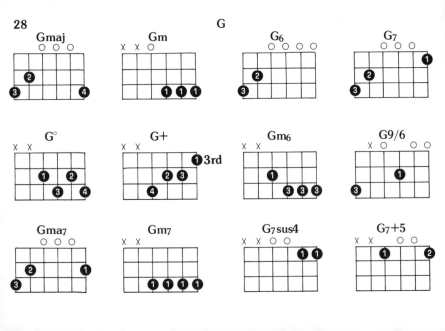

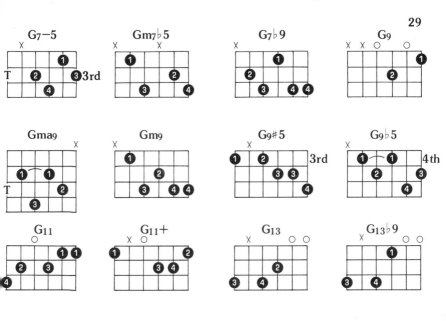

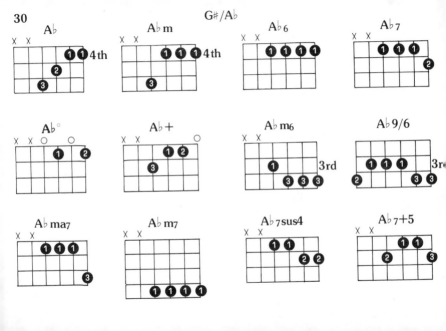

A♭7−5 A♭m7♭5 A♭7♭9 A♭9

A♭ma9 A♭m9 A♭9♯5 A♭9♭5

A♭11 A♭11+ A♭13 A♭13♭9